Essential Stories for Junior Patriots

2nd edition, Revised, Expanded

By KrisAnne Hall

Sowing the Seeds of Liberty Series

Vol. 1

CONTENTS

DEDICATED TO:

Colton and all the young patriots who deserve the best country in the world! By God's grace, Mommy and Daddy will never stop fighting for your future.

And to:

All the Moms and Dads on the frontlines and in the shadows fighting for Liberty because our children are worth it!

My son, Colton was barely four when we were returning from a grassroots rally in Ocala, FL. He announced from the backseat "Mommy, bad guys don't like Liberty and justice for all do they?" If we teach them, they get it. Let's stop selling our children short. **Sow the seeds of Liberty** in their hearts and minds and very soon we will recapture our great American Exceptionalism.

In recent years America has taken a hard turn away from Liberty, toward the destructive ideologies of collectivism. For the enemies of Liberty to implement collectivist policies, everyday Americans must be convinced that America is a failure, that its ideals are outdated or flawed from the beginning. The most susceptible to these lies are children and students who lack a proper foundation in the truth about America's founding principles. This book is for students and their parents; it will help you to become acquainted with the principles that make America exceptional.

Socialism and all other forms of collectivism are diametrically opposed to our system of government and always result in the destruction of individual liberty. In a recent survey, 64% of Americans have a favorable view of socialism. I believe our nation truly hangs by a thread – we have already lost a generation to collectivist brainwashing. Our only hope may be to raise up a new generation of patriots armed with the truth. We must start now! Take this book and others like it and **SOW THE SEEDS OF LIBERTY** into the minds of a new generation of patriots. May God grant us a space of grace to save the greatest nation ever founded in His name. If not, may HE come quickly and deliver us from our folly!

With Love.
For our Children. For our Future.

1 LIBERTY

These stories are about America, an exceptional nation. That word exceptional means special. America is a special country. That doesn't mean that other countries aren't nice, but America has a history and a heritage like no other country. There are some very special things that make America a very special place.

One of the biggest reasons America is an exceptional nation is America has protected liberty more than any other nation. Liberty – that's why America is exceptional.

Liberty gives people the ability to be happy and live their lives the way God wants them to live. By protecting liberty, America has been blessed. America has helped many other countries and millions of people to have better lives because of Liberty. We call this American Exceptionalism – America is exceptional because she values and protects Liberty.

Liberty was so important to our founders that they went to war over it. As a matter of fact, people have been fighting for Liberty for hundreds of years. Those people understood that since Liberty was a gift from God, it is very important to protect it. There are evil and misguided people who want to control Liberty, so that they can control everyone else. People who hate Liberty and try to keep people from enjoying it are called tyrants. Tyrants are like bullies at school or on the playground. Nobody likes to have a bully push them down or tell them what to do. Our founders knew many tyrants throughout history. Our founders wanted to make sure that America was a place where Liberty could grow, and tyrants – the bullies of liberty – would fail.

In some places Liberty is not protected, so people cannot experience or enjoy their Liberty. Liberty is an important gift from God, so we really need to understand what the idea of Liberty means.

John Adams and other founders of our nation believed that because we are created in the image of God, we inherited certain things from God. Sort of like how you have eyes like your mom or hair like your dad, you have inherited those things from your parents. Founders like John Adams believed you have inherited freedom from our Creator. Freedom is a very big word that has a whole lot of responsibility that goes with it. Complete freedom is something that people do not handle very well. Think about it. If you have complete freedom, then you can do whatever you want, even bad things. Our founders understood that God knows that people could not live together and be kind to one another with complete freedom, so God also gave us Law. What kind of Law did God give us? God said, that we must not steal, we must not murder, we must not lie, and so on. We call this morality, the understanding of right and wrong. So where does Liberty fit in? Liberty is that freedom we have inherited from God combined with morality so we can be a nation of good, moral people. That is what our founders believed.

Our founders knew that our country could not last long, unless we have strong morals. Because Liberty is part freedom and part morality, we could not have Liberty in America with the people ignoring one half of the equation.

Why is Liberty so important? Liberty is what allows people to believe in God the way they think is best. Liberty is what allows people to have the opportunity to be whatever they want to be when they grow up. Liberty is what allows parents to teach their children the ideas that are important to them. Liberty is what keeps the government from telling people what kind of job they must have or what they must learn and know or buy. In a society that does not have Liberty, your parents could not read to you stories like this one, they would only read stories approved by the bullies. Not only is Liberty important because it gives people the right to choose their life, it is important because it is a gift from God. Do you remember we said that we inherit Liberty from God? God gave us life, and so he gave us Liberty, too. We should never think a gift from God is not important. We must always protect the gifts that God gives us. This has been a strong belief of all the founders of our nation for hundreds of years. This is the very first part of what makes America an Exceptional Nation.

Study Questions

1. What does the word exceptional mean?
2. Why is America an exceptional nation?
3. What is a tyrant and what does a tyrant want to do?
4. Why is liberty so important?
5. Since liberty is freedom plus morality, why are both parts so important?

2 BULLY KINGS

A long time ago, nations were ruled by kings. Kings became kings when one king died and another family member took his place. Kings were always related to one another. Sometimes when a king died, he had no son to take his place. When this happened it could cause very big problems.

The history of America and its founding documents begins In England. When Edward, King of England was about to die, he had no son. King Edward had a choice to make. Should he say that his best friend, Harold, should be king? Or, should he pick his cousin William of Normandy to be the next king? King Edward picked his friend Harold. This made his cousin very angry. William of Normandy believed that since he was more closely related to King Edward, he should be king. William of Normandy had a nickname, William the Conqueror, because he was a very good soldier and had a very strong army. So, William of Normandy started a war with England. At the <u>Battle of Hastings</u> in the year 1066, William invaded and defeated England. After William's army defeated Harold's army, William was made King of England.

At this time, England already had a government with laws. The people knew that it was wrong to charge people high taxes without their permission. The people knew that it was wrong for Judges to ignore the laws and the truth and make decisions in favor of their friends and people with power. The people also knew that it was wrong for the king to take their land away from them by force or threat, only to give that land to the king's foreign friends. The people knew that these are the things that bully kings do. The people knew that people should not have to be ruled by a bully king. But when William of Normandy became King of England, he did all of these things. William of Normandy was a bully king.

There was coming a time when someone would take William's place on the throne. Instead on no sons, he had four sons! His first son, Richard, was killed in a hunting accident. So when King William died, his second son, Robert became king. Robert was a bully king too. He bullied the people just like his father. But a few good things were about to happen for the people.

King Robert wanted to be a soldier. He wanted to fight in battles more than he wanted to be king. So, King Robert left England to fight in the war of the Crusades. This meant that one of his other brothers, either William II or Henry I had to take over as king. When there are two brothers who can be king, the oldest brother gets to be king first. That meant that William II would be king before Henry I. We will never know what kind of King William II would have been, because there was a terrible accident.

One day, as William II and his brother Henry I were hunting, William II was killed by an arrow. Many people wondered if someone, perhaps Henry, had killed William II because he was about to be king. Some people looked at all the facts and decided that it was just an accident. Henry I, the youngest brother, became King of England.

Not everyone believed that William's death was just an accident. They wondered if people who wanted Henry I to be king, instead of his brother, had killed William II. This belief made it very hard for Henry I to be a king that was respected by the people. Henry I decided to make a promise to the people of England so that they would respect him as king.

Henry I made a promise to the people that he would not be a bully king like his father and brother. He not only made this promise to the people, he wrote it down on paper. In a document called the **1100 Charter of Liberties**, Henry I promised that he would not do the "evil" things that his father and brother did. He promised he would not "oppress" the people like his father and brother did. King Henry I promised he would not be a bully king.

The 1100 Charter of Liberties was a very important promise to the people. It was the first time that the king promised, in writing, not to be a bully king. Henry I listed several things that his father and brother did that he promised not to do. King Henry I promised not to tax the people like his father and brother. He promised to make sure that the leaders had to obey the law, the same as all people. These were very important promises. A king had never before written promises like these to the people.

The people had a king who was willing to say that the people deserved to have their Liberty protected and that kings should not be bullies. The people were just now beginning to understand how important Liberty is. This is the beginning of the history that would later make America an exceptional nation.

Study Questions

1. How did a person normally become king?
2. How did William of Normandy become king?
3. How did Henry I become King?
4. What did Henry I do so that the people would support him as king?
5. Why was the 1100 Charter of Liberties so unique and what were some of the promises it contained?

3 THE 1100 CHARTER OF LIBERTIES AND THE MAGNA CARTA

The 1100 Charter of Liberties made a promise of Liberty to the people. This promise was a guarantee to the people that kings should never be bullies and the people should always have Liberty. Bully kings would come again. But now the people had a guarantee in writing, and people could keep it as a reminder of their promise of Liberty.

Just about 100 years after King Henry I made his promise to the people, the people had to defend Liberty once again. The new king, King John, was a bully king. Some people say he was the biggest bully of all the kings of England. He tried to take all the people's money and their land and give to his friends. The people were very upset.

King John was the first king to create an income tax, a tax on the money people earned from their work. King John was a greedy man, and all he wanted was more and more of the people's money. Even worse than taking their money, King John would punish people if they could not pay their taxes. He was very mean and very violent. There was one very good thing, the people had the 1100 Charter of Liberties and knew that what the king was doing was evil.

Taking the people's money and punishing those who could not pay was not the only evil thing King John did. King John also wanted to tell all the people that they had to worship God his way. Archbishop Steven Langton was chosen to be the leader of the Church in England, but the king said no. Stephen Langton knew this was wrong. Mr. Langton got together with the people to fight against the king. When the men got together, they wrote down their complaints against the king. This document is called the <u>Magna Carta of 1215</u>.

The Magna Carta was a very important document. It made the king promise to let twenty-five men stop the king from being a bully. These men, chosen by the people, would watch everything the king did. When the king tried to be a bully the men could tell the king he was wrong. The king was not very happy about this. He did not want anyone to tell him what he could or could not do. Mr. Langton and the people had to start a revolution to force the king to keep the promise written in the 1100 Charter of Liberties. And when the people won the battle, the king also had to sign the Magna Carta of 1215, which told him HOW to keep his promise and how not to be a bully.

The Magna Carta was not only important to the people who were alive in 1215, it is also important to us. The Magna Carta said the people had the right to have a voice in the kingdom. This voice was the beginning of a government that represented the people. The people were beginning to understand that if they didn't want to have a bully king, they had to be a part of their own government. The people had learned that Liberty had to be protected from bully kings. They learned that if they wanted to enjoy the Liberty that God gave them, they would have to always watch the government to make sure it wasn't becoming a bully. The Magna Carta is so important to us because it was the beginning of the kind of government that makes America an Exceptional nation.

After King John made his promise in the Magna Carta of 1215, the kings did not keep this promise for very long. The people had to keep fighting against the bully kings for many years. Kings didn't like having people tell them what to do. Kings believed that they knew best and the people were not smart enough to know what was best. Kings wanted to take the people's money and spend it. Kings wanted to take people's land and use it. Kings wanted to make people think and believe only the thing that the king thought was best. These kings were bullies! A leader who does the things these bully kings did is called a tyrant. His bullying is called tyranny.

The people were learning that some kings wanted to be bullies. They were also learning that the people didn't have to put up with bully kings. They did not have to put up with tyrants or tyranny! They were beginning to see that Liberty was worth fighting for and every time they fought for Liberty, they won! This is the beginning of the lessons that will teach our founders the principles that will make America Exceptional.

Study Questions

1. What were some things King John was doing to break the promises in the 1100 Charter of Liberties?
2. When the people's religious liberty was interfered with they decided enough was enough. What document did they draft to restrain the king?
3. What are some things that tyrants do?
4. What did the people discover they had to do if they did not want tyrants to govern them?
5. What is tyranny and can you think of some modern examples?

4 BILL OF RIGHTS OF 1689

In 1626 a bully king named Charles was trying to force people to pay a tax so that he could spend the money however he wanted. He called it a "compulsory loan". But the people knew it was not a loan because the king would never pay it back. Then the king also passed a law called a "martial law" that put the king's soldiers in charge of the people. The king told his soldiers, through this martial law, to put people in jail if they refused to pay the tax. The people were not even given a trial.

The people and their representatives in government wrote a document called the **Petition of Rights**. This document reminded Charles that the Magna Carta said he could not do these things. The Petition of Rights made the king angry. He did not like the people telling him what he could and could not do. He was a bully king! He was a tyrant! When Charles refused to sign the Petition, the people and their representatives said that they would demand the king be kicked off the throne. When the bully king realized that the people were going to fight him for Liberty, he gave up and signed the Petition. This Petition made the king say that he would guarantee the people the same Liberty that the Magna Carta promised them.

But after a little while, Charles would ignore his promise and the people would have to fight again. Charles made all the representatives of the people go home. The bully king said that if the representatives would not do what he wanted, then he would make the decisions on his own. He said he didn't need them. He would not let the people have a voice in their government. He was violating the Magna Carta, he was a tyrant. In 1641, the people got together and wrote a letter called the **Grand Remonstrance**.

The Grand Remonstrance listed all the things that Charles was doing to prevent the people from enjoying Liberty. The people did not like the king taking the land away from the people for use by the king. The people knew it was wrong for the king to tell the people how to use their own land. They did not like the king trying to take their right to have guns. The people did not like the king trying to control the value of money by making coins out of metal other than gold and silver. The people knew these were the actions of a bully king, a tyrant. They knew the king was trying to keep them from enjoying their Liberty. The people declared Civil War and began to fight the king. Once again, the people pledged their lives for Liberty.

The people fought the Charles and his army from 1648 to 1649. The bully king was charged with crimes against the people's Liberty and was found guilty. Liberty won again! The people knew that tyranny was wrong, and they were willing to fight for Liberty. **The Petition of Rights and the Grand Remonstrance** became two of the documents that promised Liberty to the people and their children. Promises that our founders remembered and used when it was their time to stand against a bully king named George.

The fight for Liberty was not over. Another bully king rose up against the people in 1688. This bully king's name was James II. James II did many of the things the other bully kings did. He tried to keep the people from worshiping God the way they wanted to. He tried to change the laws of England to be the same as foreign laws that don't support Liberty. He raised taxes without the giving the people a voice in the government. He even tried to take away their right to have guns. The people knew their history and knew that James II was a bully king, he was a tyrant!

The people came together to fight this bully king. History not only showed them what a bully king looked like, but that bully kings always lose when the people stand for Liberty. The people wrote a declaration called **the Bill of Rights of 1689**. This declaration told the king everything he was doing that made him a tyrant. It also told the king that the people were not going to put up with being bullied by the king. The people were going to stand for Liberty. This time, the fight for Liberty was shorter than before. The people were so strong and fought so hard for Liberty that the king actually ran away!

The people learned that they could stand against any tyrant. They had learned that Liberty is worth fighting for. They learned that Liberty always beats tyranny, even when the bully king is very powerful. The fight may last a long time and may be hard, but they knew sooner or later Liberty would win. This is the history of our founders. This is the history that gave our founders the courage to fight the most powerful tyrant in the world. This is the history that makes America's fight for Liberty exceptional.

Study Questions

1. What were some of the things Charles I was doing to cause the people to fight back and issue the Petition of Rights?
2. Why do you think Charles called his tax a loan and why was it not a loan?
3. What were some of the complaints listed in the Grand Remonstrance?
4. Why do you think people wanted their money to be gold and silver instead of other materials like brass or paper?
5. What did the people learn from their battles with these bully kings?

5 THE LAMP OF EXPERIENCE

People have been fighting for Liberty for a very long time. Our founders knew this. They remembered, as you have read, that people in England had to defeat a bully king named William of Normandy. This king hated that the people had Liberty and made laws to keep people from enjoying their Liberty. He took away their land, their right to a fair trial, and made the people of England live under laws that prevented them from enjoying the Liberty that they knew was theirs. King William also had a son, named Robert that ruled the kingdom the same way. But when King William's son Henry I became king, he agreed to not stop them from enjoying their Liberty. To be sure that the king would keep his promise, the king signed a document called the **1100 Charter of Liberties**. This was the very first document where the government promised not to prevent people from enjoying their Liberty. The people were very happy.

It was not long before the people had to fight for Liberty again. Our founders knew that the bullies that hate Liberty never go away. They just wait for a time when they can be bullies again. King James was another bully who didn't like Liberty. He wanted to tell the people how they could worship God. He said that they could only worship God the way he wanted them to, keeping people from enjoying their Religious Liberty. A brave man, Arch Bishop Steven Langton, loved his Religious Liberty and decided that he was not going to let the king keep people from enjoying this important part of Liberty. He gathered the people together and they forced the king into accepting their Religious Liberty. Mr. Langton and his group of men wrote the **Magna Carta of 1215**. The Magna Carta was an even better promise than the Charter of Liberties.

Our founders fought again for many years to stop bully kings from keeping the people from enjoying Liberty. Over those many years, each time the people fought for the Liberty God had given them, they were able to defeat the bully kings. Each time they defeated the bully king, they got an even better promise of protection for Liberty. When the Magna Carta was violated the people drafted the **Petition of Rights** of 1628, then the **Grand Remonstrance of 1641**. The people were understanding more and more what their rights were. Every time they drafted another charter of liberty, they weakened the power of the king to rob them of their liberty. Some would say that these are just pieces of paper, but our founders called them "sentinels." These documents made it clear to the people what their rights are and how they should be protected. They gave the people hope. They gave the people clarity, direction and above all, gave them the motivation to fight for what was rightfully theirs. That is why tyrants hate documents like these, and by the way, that's a good way to spot a tyrant!

When it came time for our founders to fight for Liberty, they knew just how to do it. They learned from their history and knew that the king did not have the right to keep people from enjoying the Liberty that God had given them. Their fathers had just finished fighting the king in the **Glorious Revolution of 1688**. Their fathers had made the king and Queen promise to always protect the Liberty of the people. The King and Queen made this promise in the **Bill of Rights of 1689**. So when the new king, King George III, refused to keep the promises in the Bill of Rights of 1689, our founders knew they had to fight for Liberty again. Our founders loved their country of England. They did not want to fight the country they had been raised to know as their own. But they knew that if they did not stand against this bully king, then they would not be able to enjoy their Liberty and the king would bully them and keep them from their rights forever. Our founders demanded their Liberty. Founder Richard Henry Lee wrote a plan called the Lee Resolution. On June 6, 1776 his plan was adopted by the men who were willing to fight for Liberty. The founders agreed that Mr. Lee's plan was the best. This plan said all the colonies were free from the laws of England and from the tyrant, King George. They were now thirteen separate countries. The plan also made the colonies promise to work together to get help from foreign friends. They also knew they had to join together as one group of States so they could protect each other and work together to make a great nation.

Our founders had the courage to stand against this bully king and fight for the Liberty that God gave them. This is what makes America an Exceptional Nation.

Study Questions

1. Name five documents that helped shape the foundations of our American Constitution.
2. What resolution officially put America on the path to independence from Great Britain?
3. What was the latest major document from the king that our founders had in the colonies which declared their rights as Englishmen?

Project:

Compare the Declaration of Independence with the English Bill of Rights of 1689. What similarities do you see? How similar are the preceding four documents?

6 SAMUEL ADAMS

Our founders believed that Liberty was so important that they promised their lives, all their money and possessions, and their very reputations. They promised to fight for Liberty until the very end. Our founders could not understand why England, the country they loved so dearly, would want to hurt them by trying to keep them from enjoying their natural rights.

For many years they wrote letters to King George and to Parliament asking them to keep their promise and to protect the Liberty that belonged to the people. They asked the king to stop taxing them without giving them a voice in their government. They asked the king to stop forcing them to buy certain products. They asked King George to stop making his soldiers search their homes and take their things. They asked the king to keep his promise. They knew they had a right to own guns, to share their ideas, to worship God, and the right to a jury trial. The king refused or ignored every single request of the people of the colonies.

George continued to go against every promise in the Bill of Rights of 1689. So some of the men and women of the American Colonies knew that they had to take a stand against King George, or they would soon have nothing and have no ability to enjoy their Liberty.

Samuel Adams was one of the leaders who wanted to stop the bully king. In 1743, Mr. Adams asked people if it was wrong to fight against a tyrant if there is no other way to keep Liberty? Sam Adams knew that the people could not be breaking the law if they were standing for Liberty! He realized that it was the king who was breaking the law, because he was not following the written documents that told the king to protect Liberty!

In 1763 King George III announced that England would tax the colonies to pay for the war that had been fought. The king also began telling the colonist what they had to buy and what they could not buy. Sam Adams organized groups of men to protest the bully king's taxes and mandates. Mr. Adams knew when the king took money away from the people, that he was really taking their power and their voice. When the king took the power and the voice from the people, he was only doing it so he could have all the power for himself. Sam Adams warned the people that if they let the king tax their hard work, he will tax their land. He said if the king is allowed to tax our land, he will tax everything we have. Mr. Adams believed that if the government could take away money and property from the people, then they would no longer be free, but would be slaves.

Samuel Adams and his friends formed groups called **Committees of Correspondence** that taught many people about the value of Liberty and how the king was trying to keep Liberty from the people. Over the next few months more than 100 other groups were formed in the towns and villages of Massachusetts, all ready to protest the evil work of this bully king. These groups eventually spread all over the colonies, and people would learn what their own government was doing to take away Liberty. Sam Adams knew if they did not fight tyranny now, people in the future would not have Liberty. Our founders were not only fighting for their Liberty, but for the Liberty of generations to come. That included you and your family. Imagine, someone fighting that long ago, 1763, for your Liberty today! How many years ago was that? It is amazing that Sam Adams and his friends thought that far ahead. They knew they had to fight for themselves AND for all the people who would come after them.

In 1773, Samuel Adams and his group, The Sons of Liberty, held a huge protest of the king's tyrannical actions. These groups decided to protest the taxes and the mandates that the king was placing on them. They organized groups all along the east coast of the new colonies to dump tea into the ocean, all at the same time. The most famous of these protests was the Boston Tea Party. During this protest, Samuel Adams and his group of men dressed up like American Indians and dumped all the tea that was sitting on ship into the Boston Harbor.

Another way Sam Adams fought for Liberty was by writing many essays and articles. One of his essays he wrote for a newspaper said the only way we can really enjoy Liberty is if we are a moral people. Do you remember that Liberty is freedom plus morality? Mr. Adams was reminding us that Liberty has two parts. Liberty cannot last without both parts together. Sam Adams was very passionate about Liberty and knew that our founders were fighting for something that was very important

Samuel Adams did not stop his fight for Liberty in the Boston Harbor. Mr. Adams kept his promise. He sacrificed everything he had for Liberty. Samuel Adams kept serving the cause of Liberty throughout his life. Over Samuel Adam's life, the people continued to choose him as a representative of the people. He served as the clerk of the Massachusetts House of Representatives, a delegate from Massachusetts to the Continental Congress, the President of the Massachusetts Senate, Third Lieutenant Governor of Massachusetts, and the fourth Governor of Massachusetts. Because of men and women like Samuel and Elizabeth Adams, sacrificing their entire lives for Liberty, America was able to be an Exceptional Nation.

Study Questions

1. What were the colonists asking King George to stop doing?
2. Of the parties involved in the struggle for liberty, who was engaging in lawlessness?
3. What prompted the men to dump tea all along the east coast?
4. What were the Committees of Correspondence? Are you aware of any groups like this today?
5. Describe the extensive career that Sam Adams had in American government.

7 PATRIOTS OF COLOR

As we learn about the history that makes America an exceptional nation, we must not forget our men and women of color. It should not be surprising to know that men of color fought in the revolutionary war. They knew that the bully king would never let all men have Liberty; he would never let all men be free. They believed in Liberty and knew that America was a place where all men could eventually be free. They picked up arms to help overthrow the bully king and if we forget this part of our history, we will never understand the true meaning of American Exceptionalism. These men were recognized for their bravery and their courage. Our story must begin with Crispus Attucks.

Crispus Attucks was a slave who became a wailer with the merchant marines in the Boston Harbor, as soon as he was a freeman. One day there was a loud ringing of bells. Mr. Attucks thought there was a fire. He ran out of his ship to find that the bells were calling to Patriots to fight against the bully king. Without a single thought of his own safety, Mr. Attucks ran back into the ship and got 55 men to join him in the battle for Liberty. Mr. Attucks knew he had to fight for Liberty. Since he used to be a slave, he knew that Liberty was the most important thing. The king's soldiers were waiting for them and Mr. Attucks was shot and killed. It is believed he was the first Patriot to die for the holy cause of Liberty in America.

Mr. John Boyle O'Reilly wrote a poem about Mr. Attucks. In his poem he said:

"Honor to Crispus Attucks, who was leader and voice that day;
The first to defy, and the first to die, with Maverick, Carr, and Gray.
Call it riot or revolution, his hand first clenched at the crown:
His feet were the first in perilous place to pull the King's flag down:
His breast was the first one rent apart that liberty's stream might flow;
For our freedom now and forever, his head was the first laid low.
Call it riot or revolution, or mob or crowd, as you may,
such deaths have been seed of nations, such lives shall be honored for aye."

Mr. Attucks was not the only hero that was a man of color, many men of color formed the Bucks of America, a militia from the state of Massachusetts. George Middleton was a freeman and a man of color. He volunteered to be a leader in the fight for Liberty from the bully king. Mr. Middleton was given the rank of Colonel in his army called the Bucks of America. He continued the fight for Liberty after the Revolutionary War by forming the African Benevolent Society in 1796, which provided assistance to widows and orphans.

Peter Salem, a slave, told his master that he wanted to fight for Liberty against King George. Mr. Salem was declared a freeman because he wanted to fight for Liberty! Peter Salem joined the Continental Army. He fought at Bunker Hill where he is remembered for shooting and killing British Major John Pitcairn. Many believe if it had not been for Peter Salem, Major Pitcairn would have won the battle. Peter Salem was so loved by the soldiers of New England that they gave Mr. Salem an award for his bravery, and he was introduced to General George Washington as a great hero. Peter Salem continued to fight for Liberty and fought bravely in many battles.

Let's meet another hero in the American Revolution, his name is Ned Hector. Mr. Hector was another patriot of color who fought in the battles at Brandywine and Germantown. Mr. Hector is remembered for his great bravery. When his military unit was being defeated and the order to retreat was given, he would not run away. He did not want the bully king's army to get his horses and weapons. He said, "The enemy shall not have my team. I will save the horses or perish myself." He was willing to give his life for Liberty.

Admiral Bernardo de Galvez, was a great leader and fighter for Liberty and the Governor of Louisiana when it was owned by Spain. Admiral de Galvez smuggled items into the colonies to help the people fight against the bully king. He risked his life and his sailors to bring the people gunpowder, muskets, uniforms, medicine and other supplies. Before the country of Spain ever decided to help the colonists in the war, Admiral de Galvez was fighting in New Orleans for Liberty! Admiral de Galvez captured a letter from the bully king that told the king's General exactly where to attack the colonists. Admiral Galvez took this letter and quickly organized the troops to defend Louisiana. They were able to kick the British soldiers out of the Mississippi River and out of Mobile, Alabama. Admiral Bernardo de Galvez fought bravely for the colonists and helped them stop the bully king!

Our founding fathers fought for a nation where it is known that all people are created equal. They knew that God created everyone in His image and gave everyone the right of life, liberty, and the pursuit of happiness. These brave and heroic men of color believed in this nation of Liberty, too. They pledged their lives because they knew that if Liberty would win, they would be part of a nation where Liberty would grow and everyone would eventually be free. Men and women of all color and nations joined in this battle for Liberty. That is why America is an Exceptional nation.

Study Questions

1. Who was the first man killed in the battle for independence?
2. How did Peter Salem contribute to the fight for independence?
3. Who was George Middleton?
4. Name two significant battles in which the brave patriot Ned Hector fought.
5. How did Admiral Bernardo de Galvez contribute to the fight for independence?

8 JAMES OTIS, JR.

As the King George and his government became more and more evil, they started using British soldiers to keep people from enjoying their Liberty. King George and his government had written a law called the Writs of Assistance. Writs of Assistance gave the soldiers the power to force their way into people's homes and businesses to search for things that they could take from the colonists. The soldiers could tell the people they were looking for things that broke the law, even if they were not. If the people said no, then the soldiers would arrest them and put them in jail. One man stood against them. That man was James Otis, Jr.

James Otis, Jr. was the oldest of thirteen children. Can you imagine having twelve brothers and sisters? Mr. Otis' father was very patriotic and raised his children to stand for what is right. Mr. Otis's sister, Mercy Otis Warren was very important to the founding of America, too. James Otis, Sr. was a lawyer and James Otis, Jr. grew up to be a lawyer, also. James. Otis, Jr. used his profession to fight the bully king and his laws that hurt the people and tried to take away their Liberty.

When the bully king passed a law that took the people's money through taxes, the people were very upset. The people protested and refused to agree to the law. The bully king used a bully law called Writs of Assistance to come into people's homes businesses, ships, and buildings. The soldiers did not have to warn the people that they were coming. The soldiers could go anywhere they wanted to go, look through people's things, and take them to jail. The soldiers didn't even have to have a real reason to do what they did. The soldiers then became the bullies working for a bully king.

James Otis, Jr. knew this law was wrong. The king was breaking the promise he made to the people in the Bill of Rights of 1689. Mr. Otis loved his native country of England. Because he loved his country he could not let his people suffer at the hand of the bully king. In February of 1761, Mr. Otis argued in the State House for five hours that these Writs of Assistance were against the English law.

Mr. Otis told everyone that the Writs of Assistant were going to kill Liberty and destroy the very basis for English law. He knew that the most important kind of Liberty was to be free and safe in your own home. He knew that the Bill of Rights of 1689 was a promise from the king to never search the people without warning or without a good reason. He knew that the bully king was breaking that promise, and James Otis, Jr. had to stand against this tyranny or Liberty would be lost forever.

Some people today say that what James Otis Jr. did was no big deal. That's not what those who were there said. Here is what John Adams said about that day:

"But Otis was a flame of fire! With a promptitude of classical allusions, a depth of research, a rapid summary of historical events and dates, a profusion of legal authorities, a prophetic glare of his eyes into (the future), and a rapid torrent of impetuous eloquence, he hurried away all before him. * American Independence was then and there born. The seeds of Patriots and Heroes — to defend the vigorous youth, were then and there sown. Every man of an immense, crowded audience, appeared to me to go away, as I did, ready to take arms against Writs of Assistance. Then, and there, was the first scene of the first act of opposition to the arbitrary claims of Great Britain — then and there, the child Independence was born. In fifteen years, i.e. in 1776, he grew up to man hood, and declared himself free."

As Mr. Otis stood for Liberty, against the bully laws, people all around threatened him, lied about him, and called him bad names, like traitor. That did not stop Mr. Otis. He decided that standing for Liberty was more important than people liking him or calling him names. He said that the only thing that really mattered to a person who loved God and loved Liberty was what he could do for the Liberty of his country.

After his argument against Writs of Assistance, Mr. Otis continued to fight for Liberty. He was a leader for the Stamp Act Congress, wrote several important patriotic pamphlets, and on September 12, 1768 gave a very important speech at a town hall meeting, encouraging others to fight for Liberty.

James Otis, Jr. was not afraid of anything that a man could say or do against him. He knew that Liberty was a gift from God and there is nothing more important than standing for the things that God has given to us. James Otis, Jr. pledged his life, his home, his health and his reputation, even when people lied and called him bad names. Because of people like James Otis, Jr., who loved Liberty more than their own lives, America was able to become an exceptional nation.

Study Questions

1. What were the Writs of Assistance?
2. Are there laws today that bear any resemblance to the Writs of Assistance?
3. What amendment in the Bill of rights protects you from the government coming into your home or taking your property without a warrant?
4. How significant was James Otis Jr.'s stand to John Adams and the men that lived through these events?
5. The struggle for Liberty took a serious toll on the health of James Otis, Jr. What would you be willing to give to protect Liberty?

9 RICHARD HENRY LEE

Richard Henry Lee was a very important founder of our exceptional nation. Mr. Lee was born January 20, 1732 in Westmorland, Virginia. His family had been in Virginia for many generations. Mr. Lee attended school in England and was an exceptional student. As soon as he was finished with school he returned to his home in the colonies.

In 1751 he formed his own troop to try and fight in the French and Indian war. In 1757, Richard Henry Lee was chosen to sit on the House of Burgesses, the first group of elected Englishmen in the colonies. Mr. Lee was so shy, that he didn't really say much, until one day. In 1765, another Patriot by the name of Patrick Henry told everyone about the bully king's Stamp tax. Mr. Henry told the people how they could end the tyranny of the king. Patrick Henry was said to be such a great speaker that he could make people want to be involved. This is what happened to Richard Henry Lee. Before Mr. Lee knew it, he was so excited about what Patrick Henry was saying that he jumped in and stared to speak alongside Mr. Henry.

Richard Henry Lee did such a great job helping Patrick Henry that it was not long before they had enough people to stand against the bully king. Patrick Henry and Richard Henry Lee's work would force the king to take back the Stamp tax. The people had discovered that the Stamp tax not only taxed paper, but removed the colonist's right to a trial by their peers.

Mr. Lee also joined with the patriot, Samuel Adams to form a group of people who would tell colonists the truth about the bully king. So many times the bully king would try to trick the people and hide the bad things he was doing to Liberty. These groups worked hard to watch the bully king and his Government so the people could know the truth. They named their groups, Committees of Correspondence. Richard Henry Lee and Samuel Adams had the courage to be great leaders and were able to bring the people together and give them the truth. They told the colonists how to fight their government as it became more and more of a tyrant over the people.

Mr. Lee was not done with his patriotic duty. In 1774 he was elected to become Virginia's representative to the Continental Congress. It was during the second meeting of this Congress, that people knew that things were not going to get better between the colonies and their government in England. The king and the government refused to allow the people to enjoy the Liberty that God had given them. The Government made more and more laws that made the colonists more like slaves and less like free people. On June 7, 1776, Richard Henry Lee, who was a great speaker, told the Congress about his Lee Resolution that said the colonies had a right to be free, and that they would not be a part of England any more.

Richard Henry Lee continued to serve the people of the United States of America. He was actually the fourth President under the Articles of Confederation, our country's first Constitution. He also served as a Senator to the state of Virginia until 1792, when he retired. Mr. Lee had given so much of himself to the cause of Liberty that he became sick and he couldn't be a Senator. Patrick Henry said that anyone who heard Mr. Lee speak believed that there was no one who was a better speaker. His love for Liberty was remembered by all who knew him. It is because of Richard Henry Lee's love of and lifelong devotion to Liberty, that we were able to create the United States of America, an exceptional nation.

Study Question

1. Who made the proposal for Independence in 1776?
2. What helped motivate Richard Henry Lee to speak out?
3. What other important jobs did Richard Henry Lee have in trying to build a great nation?
4. Did America have presidents before George Washington?
5. What finally cause Richard Henry Lee to resign his job representing the people?

10 PATRICK HENRY

Patrick Henry was an exceptional man of passion and courage. Mr. Henry was born in Virginia May 29, 1736 and was homeschooled by his father. Mr. Henry tried very hard to be a successful business man, but God had other plans for Patrick Henry. After two business failed, Mr. Henry decided he wanted to become a lawyer. He taught himself how to be a lawyer and convinced attorneys in Virginia that he would be a good lawyer. Mr. Henry did become a very good lawyer.
In 1765, Mr. Henry joined Richard Henry Lee in the House of Burgesses. Mr. Henry had won a very important legal case that proved to people that he was a great speaker and a smart man who believed in the right things. This was the same year that the king and the government of England had placed the Stamp Act on the colonies, but refused to give the Colonies any representation in government. Mr. Henry wrote a plan. He told the people that they should stand up against this bullying by the king and the government.

Mr. Henry was one of the first American Patriots brave enough to stand up against King George and his government. He was one of the first to say that people who love Liberty cannot allow their government to be a bully. Many of the people in the House of Burgesses did not like what Patrick Henry had to say. They accused him of being a traitor. Patrick Henry did not back down. He proved that he was a man who stood for Liberty, no matter what names people called him. Patrick Henry and Richard Henry Lee worked together on this plan against the king's law.

The Boston Massacre was where British soldiers shot and killed three people. Patrick Henry helped organize groups of people in the colonies to inform the colonists. They named their groups, Committees of Correspondence. The Committees helped to teach the people and bring them together for Liberty. These committees were in all the colonies. They worked together to show the colonist how the government was bullying the people. Remember, this bullying is what we call tyranny.

In 1774 Mr. Henry was chosen to represent the people of Virginia in the Continental Congress. He worked very hard to unite the people as Americans and stand against the tyranny of their government in England. He gave a speech that told the people that they were ALL AMERICANS! The colonists used to be proud British citizens. But the tyrant king and his government's laws against Liberty were wrong. The colonists knew that they had to be Americans instead, so America could stand for Liberty.

When Mr. Henry's wife died in 1775, he spent all his time fighting for Liberty. He joined with some people who wanted to protect each other and their communities and defend Liberty. His group was called the Militia of Hanover County Virginia. In March of 1775 he was chosen to represent the people of Virginia. The people didn't know if they wanted to keep asking the king to stop being a bully, or if they wanted to fight back.

Patrick Henry believed that the king and the government were never going to listen to the people. He knew the king was not going to keep his promise in the Bill of Rights of 1689. King George would never let the people enjoy Liberty. Patrick Henry knew that people were already fighting for Liberty in their homes and on their property. He told the people that begging the king to keep his promise was a waste of time, since they had already been petitioning the king for over ten years and he wasn't listening.

Patrick Henry gave a very important speech on March 23, 1775 in a place called Saint John's Church. He asked the people why they were just sitting around while others had to fight for Liberty. He could not understand how people could sit by and watch the king bully their neighbors. He knew that if they did not fight back now, everyone would become a slave to the bully king. He told the people that he would fight. He knew that Liberty was the most important thing and shouted "give me Liberty or give me death." Patrick Henry knew that without Liberty, life was slavery, and it was not worth living.

After the people won the war against their government, Patrick Henry continued to fight to protect Liberty by working very hard for a Bill of Rights. The Bill of Rights would list some of the rights that are held by the people. It made the government promise to never to do anything to interfere with these rights.

One right that was very important to Patrick Henry is protected by the Second Amendment in the Bill of Rights. This is the Amendment that says that the government can never interfere with citizens owning guns. Mr. Henry believed this was the most important right. He stood up against a man named Edmund Pendleton who thought Mr. Henry was being silly. Mr. Pendleton believed that the people could stop tyrants from bullying the citizens just by talking to them or removing them from office. This idea made Patrick Henry very upset. He said, "O sir, we would have fine times, indeed, if, to punish tyrants, it were only sufficient to assemble the people! Your arms, wherewith you could defend yourself are gone. Did you ever read of any revolution in a nation inflicted by those who had no power at all?" Patrick Henry and our founders believed that the number one reason we have guns is to protect ourselves from a bully government who want to rob us of our liberty.

Thanks to men like Patrick Henry, James Madison, and John Leland, we have a Bill of Rights. Our Bill of Rights reminds every American that God gave them Liberty and it is the Government's job to protect that Liberty. Without Patrick Henry's love and sacrifice for Liberty, even our founders would agree that we would not have beaten the tyrant king and his government. We would not live in a country that knows Liberty should be defended at all hazards. This is just one more reason why America is such an exceptional nation.

Study Questions

1. What right did Patrick Henry think was the most important for making sure Liberty survived?
2. Where did Patrick Henry go to school?
3. How did Patrick Henry become a lawyer?
4. Where did Patrick Henry give his most famous speech?
5. Why did Patrick Henry believe people had to make sure they kept their guns?

11 JAMES MADISON

James Madison was a man of great integrity and honor. People call him the Father of the Constitution. But Mr. Madison is so much more than that. Mr. Madison, even as a young man, fought for Liberty. He worked with the people who wrote the Virginia Constitution and the Virginia Declaration of Rights. These were two documents that helped the people of Virginia remember that Liberty is a gift from God and that it is the Government's job to protect that Liberty. The people of Virginia knew they had the right to enjoy Liberty.

Mr. Madison worked hard to understand how good Governments worked. He researched many governments throughout history and knew the history of his own English government. After the American Revolution the colonies voted to have an Articles of Confederation; a Constitution that united the colonies into thirteen united states. Our founders had beaten the largest military force on the planet. They were fighting against the tyranny of a large government. They did not want to create a Constitution that gave them a government that would be a bully like the one they fought against.

When our founders created the Articles of Confederation, they made the Central Government very small, and very limited. Because James Madison studied the history of governments, he believed that the Articles would not work. He believed that it did not give the Central Government enough power to survive. He was right. The Central Government, under the Articles of Confederation was not even strong enough to pay people come to work. It failed. James Madison wanted to fix it. He did not want an overpowering central government, but he did want one that was stronger that the government under the Articles of Confederation. A long debate occurred between the Federalists and Antifederalist to find the right balance.

The representatives of the colonies met and worked very hard to write a new Constitution. Mr. Madison wanted everyone to remember how important it was for the people to have representation in the new Central Government. He also fought hard for the three branches of the Central Government to watch each other and stop each other from becoming tyrants over the people. In the end, Mr. Madison was able to teach people how important it was to create a Central Government that would protect Liberty. You can read much of what Madison said about our Constitution in the Federalist Papers.

James Madison's fight for Liberty did not end there. He worked with Thomas Jefferson and John Leland to make sure that America had a Bill of Rights that would protect Liberty for the people. Mr. Madison studied history. He knew when people enjoy Liberty for a long time, and don't have to fight to keep it, they forget how important it is. When people forget how important Liberty is, bullies work hard to keep people from enjoying Liberty. Mr. Madison wanted to make sure that when people in the future forgot how important Liberty was, they would have a Bill of Rights to remind them that Liberty belongs to the people. The people would be reminded a bully Government should never be allowed to get between people and Liberty.

James Madison won his fight for the Bill of Rights. He continued to fight for Liberty and serve the people as Secretary of State for President Thomas Jefferson. James Madison was also the fourth president of the United States and he was president for eight years. Mr. Madison was so dedicated to Liberty, that even after he retired, he started the American Colonization Society. Madison's group was dedicated to the fight to free slaves in America.

Madison was a man of true integrity and honor. He believed Liberty was more important than anything on earth. James Madison dedicated his life to the fight for Liberty. Because men like James Madison were willing to give everything they had so that all could have Liberty, America became an exceptional nation.

Study Questions

1. What other important documents, besides our Constitution, did James Madison help create?
2. Why do you think the founders made the central government so small under the Articles of Confederation?
3. What do you think the Antifederalists were worried about when the Federalist wanted to give the central government more power?
4. Where can we go to find out what Madison said about how the Constitution and the government was supposed to work?
5. What was added to the Constitution to address some of the concerns of the Antifederalist and others who wanted to protect individual rights and the freedom of the States?

12 JOHN LELAND

James Madison worked hard to give America a constitutional republic. A Constitutional Republic is a government that is run by the people, for the good of the people, and dedicated to the protection of Liberty for all. He would have never succeeded in that mission if it had not been for a man named John Leland.

John Leland was a Virginia politician and a Baptist Minister from Massachusetts. John Leland was loved by the people and they wanted him to be the representative for Virginia in the first Congress. Mr. Leland also loved Liberty and believed that all people should be able to believe in God however they want to. He was the leader of a group of men called the Virginia Baptist Convention. This group believed that the Constitution as it was planned didn't give people enough protection to believe in God as they wanted. This idea is called **Religious Liberty**. The Virginia Baptist Convention knew their history and knew how important it would be to make sure that everyone could enjoy religious Liberty.

When the people first came to the continent of America, they were looking for a place to practice their own religion. They wanted the freedom to worship God without the bully king telling them how to do it. When the colonists set up their own governments here in America, they wrote constitutions called Charters. Each Charter set up what religion would be allowed in that Charter. Anyone who wanted to have a church or preach had to get a license from the government of that Charter or be branded a criminal. Also, the Charters created a law called the Test Act. The Test Acts stated that no one could be a part of the Charter government unless they were part of the religion of that Charter. This meant they had no voice in their government. This was not religious liberty.

These government Charters created a problem for Baptist ministers and preachers. Of the original thirteen colonies, none allowed Baptists to practice their religion. These men were not only told not to preach or have church, if they tried to they were arrested, fined, imprisoned, or even killed. It is hard to believe that such things could happen here in America, but the Virginia Baptist Convention knew this history. They knew the stories about Dr. John Clarke and Obadiah Holmes. They knew the struggles of Roger Williams and of the fifty Baptist preachers jailed in Virginia. They wanted to make sure these things never happened again. John Leland believed that all people should have Liberty, "Jews, Turks, Pagans and Christians." These men understood from personal history that stopping religious Liberty was a terrible thing. They believed that God didn't need governments to force people to believe. They knew that God's Word was strong enough to convict hearts and teach the truth all by itself.

John Leland did not want to be a politician. He wanted to remain a Baptist Minister. He talked to Thomas Jefferson and James Madison about making a deal. John Leland met with James Madison and told Mr. Madison if he promised to make sure that a Bill of Rights was put into the Constitution to protect religious liberty, Mr. Leland would make sure that Mr. Madison would be the Virginia representative to the first Congress.

John Leland had to really trust James Madison to be a man of his word. Virginia wanted the Bill of Rights very badly. They were willing to vote against the Constitution and prevent the United States from happening if there was no Bill of Rights. They knew that if they elected James Madison instead of John Leland, they would have to vote for the Constitution and trust Mr. Madison to keep his word. Mr. Madison had to promise to fight for the Liberty that they knew people deserved. John Leland trusted James Madison and Mr. Madison kept his word. James Madison gathered men together to fight for religious Liberty. Richard Henry Lee joined in this fight. Mr. Lee knew that the founders had the same religious beliefs now, but they were creating a nation for the future. They knew that religious Liberty had to be a part of that plan.

John Leland loved Liberty so much that he was not willing to create a new government unless he was sure that religious Liberty was there for everyone. He fought for religious Liberty and convinced James Madison to fight for it too. If it had not been for these men fighting for religious Liberty, people would not be free to worship God the way they want to. It is because of religious Liberty that America is an exceptional nation.

Study Questions

1. What was John Leland's profession?
2. What is Religious Liberty?
3. Why were Test Acts and preaching licenses a problem for some citizens?
4. Why did Baptists in the colonies have to fight for Liberty?
5. Why was it so important for the creation of the United States for James Madison to keep his promise to John Leland?

13 FOUNDING MOTHERS

The men were not the only people who sacrificed and fought for this great nation. To understand the fight for Liberty, we must know all the people who fought for us. Our founders, both men and women, knew they were fighting to create a Nation that would last for a very long time. They wanted to make a nation that would protect Liberty for millions of people who were not even born yet. That meant they were thinking of you and me. They promised that they would sacrifice everything they had, even their own lives, just so you and I could live in a Nation where people could enjoy Liberty without being bullied by their government.

Many women fought for Liberty, too. These brave women knew that they had to stand for Liberty or their children would not be able to live in a country where Liberty could be enjoyed. When these women saw what the bully king was doing they didn't worry about themselves, but worried for the children and grandchildren. Moms think this way. One of these great women was Penelope Barker and she was the leader of the second Tea Party. Just ten months after Mr. Sam Adams and his friends dumped tea in the water, Penelope Barker asked the women to join in the fight against the bully king. She sent this message to her friends: "Maybe it has only been men who have protested the king up to now. That only means we women have taken too long to let our voices be heard."

Penelope Barker was very sad about how England was treating the colonies. She knew she had to stand for Liberty. She shared her statement with the world even though it meant she would be in danger. The women who joined Mrs. Barker were very brave and worked very hard to fight the bully king so all people could be free to enjoy Liberty. When the women made their statement to the king, they were not afraid to tell the king who they were. They knew by saying their names the king could not ignore them.

"We are signing our names to a document not hiding ourselves behind costumes like the men in Boston did at their tea party. The British will know who we are". Mrs. Barker had many friends to help her. She found women who also believed in Liberty for all. These women were willing to give their lives and their homes to the holy cause of Liberty. Elizabeth King gave her home to share in the battle for Liberty. In the home of Elizabeth King, over 50 women met and made a promise to give everything they had for the fight for Liberty. They promised to not buy anything made in England until the bully king stopped trying to take their Liberty.

These women were so angry at what King George was doing to their friends and family that they didn't care what the king would do to them. They were willing to do anything so their children could have Liberty. When these women made their promise to not buy English made things, they knew that their husbands would be in trouble and could even lose their jobs. Although they were insulted and ridiculed in the newspapers, they decided that Liberty was more important than their husbands' paychecks, or even their lives or reputations.

Mercy Otis Warren was another friend of Penelope Barker and a very brave woman. Mercy Otis Warren was a very good writer who wrote many plays and essays about Liberty, the colonies, and the fight against the bully king. Her friend, Abigail Adams, said in 1773 that Mercy was "a sincere lover of [her] country". She said Mercy Otis Warren was so sad about the king's tyranny that she wept over the bad things the king was doing.

Elizabeth Adams, wife of Samuel Adams, had to leave her home and hide to protect her family. Elizabeth and Sam Adams gave everything they had for Liberty. Elizabeth Adams even had to write letters to her husband using a broken pair of scissors as a pen and live on the run, because they had nothing left. Samuel Adams and Elizabeth Adams knew that nothing was more important than Liberty. They knew that if they did not have Liberty all the other things they had would mean nothing or be taken away by the bully king. The understood that no cost was too great to fight for Liberty and gave up everything they had.

Our founding mothers knew that they were fighting in a battle not just for themselves but for their children and grandchildren. They knew that nothing was too much to give so that the gift of Liberty could be passed on. They knew, as Mercy Otis Warren said, that if they did not stand against tyranny today, their children would bow to him tomorrow. Because these women knew how important Liberty would be for their children and gave everything they could possibly give, America was able to become an exceptional nation!

Study Questions

1. Did the women of the American colonies help found the United States of America?
2. Who organized a group of women in the home of Elizabeth King to protest the king's taxes?
3. What happened when Penelope Barker and her group published their protest?
4. What were some of the things Mercy Otis Warren did to help promote Liberty and fight the king?
5. What were some of the things Elizabeth Adams had to suffer in her fight for Liberty?

14 THOMAS JEFFERSON

Thomas Jefferson defeated John Adams to become our third President. He served our country in many ways for more than fifty years. On June 7, 1776, Richard Henry Lee wrote a plan called the Lee Resolution. The founders of America voted on Mr. Lee's plan and made it a law. Mr. Lee plan said that we should be free from the bully King, George III and that the colonies must join together to beat the bully king. Because of Mr. Lee's plan, Thomas Jefferson was asked to write the Declaration of Independence.

Thomas Jefferson was a very important founder. He was only 23 years old when he wrote the Declaration of Independence. Mr. Jefferson loved his country of England, but could not live with a bully king. He wrote a letter to a friend and said there was no one who loved England more than he did. He told his friend that he would fight before he would allow the king to bully him. He knew that many people in the colonies felt the same way.

Mr. Jefferson knew his history and knew what a bully king looked like. He wrote the Declaration of Independence to look just like the Bill of Rights of 1689! Mr. Jefferson also knew that Liberty was a gift from God. He wrote in the Declaration of Independence:

"We hold these truths to be self-evident, that all men are created equal, that they are endowed by their Creator with certain unalienable Rights that among these are Life, Liberty and the pursuit of Happiness."

He also believed that the "the Laws of Nature and of Nature's God" gave people the right to be free. In the Declaration of Independence, Mr. Jefferson also made a plea to God to help them fight for Liberty with the "protection of Divine Providence."

Mr. Jefferson knew that he could not sit and allow a bully king to take this gift of God from the people. The people of the colonies had asked the king over and over to keep his promise to protect Liberty. The king ignored them and the promises he made. He kept making laws against Liberty and forcing the people to obey. The king had even begun to use his soldiers to enforce these laws that hurt the people and their Liberty. Mr. Jefferson wrote in the Declaration of Independence:

"In every stage of these Oppressions We have Petitioned for Redress in the most humble terms: Our repeated Petitions have been answered only by repeated injury. A Prince whose character is thus marked by every act which may define a Tyrant, is unfit to be the ruler of a free people."

Thomas Jefferson and the people of the colonies knew that a bully king could never be the leader of a people who wanted Liberty. He believed that if the people stood against the bully king, God would protect the people and let them see Liberty again. But he wanted to warn us, that we must remember that Liberty is a gift from God. He was afraid that if people forgot that, that Liberty would be easily controlled by a bully king. He was sad for his country England, because they had forgotten this important truth. He knew that God would stand with the people who stood with Liberty and punish those who did not.

Thomas Jefferson said, "And can the liberties of a nation be thought secure when we have removed their only firm basis, a conviction in the minds of the people that these liberties are the gift of God? That they are not to be violated but with his wrath? Indeed I tremble for my country when I reflect that God is just: that his justice cannot sleep forever." Our founders, like Thomas Jefferson, knew that God gave us Liberty and that we must fight for Liberty to be good stewards of all that we have been given.

Thomas Jefferson's father, Peter was a successful farmer and surveyor with a large amount of land. Thomas Jefferson inherited much of this land and began building his home, Monticello. You can visit Monticello today and see where Jefferson lived. Jefferson was a compassionate man. He inherited slaves from his father. He freed seven of them. He did not go after two that ran away. Another five, he put in his will.

In addition to serving as President, Jefferson served in as governor in Virginia, as trade commissioner and minister to France (replacing Ben Franklin). In 1790 he served under his friend George Washington as Secretary of State, where he spent most of his time fighting the policies of Alexander Hamilton which he thought favored the British too much.

While Jefferson was President he oversaw the Louisiana Purchase and supported Lewis and Clark's expedition. When his friend James Madison became president after him, he retired to Monticello and sold his large collection of books to the government to start the Library of Congress. He and his close friend John Adams died on the same day, July 4th, 1826, the 50th anniversary of the Declaration of Independence.

Great men like Thomas Jefferson fighting for what is right is what makes America an Exceptional nation.

Study Questions

1. What famous document did Thomas Jefferson write?
2. What document does the Declaration of Independence closely resemble?
3. What did Thomas Jefferson believe we must remember if our Liberty is to remain secure?
4. What were some of the offices that Thomas Jefferson held?
5. When did Jefferson die?

15 GEORGE WASHINGTON

George Washington was a man of great character. Even though he was often sick, he was a strong and courageous man. Some people say that his desire to fight for Liberty was part of his family heritage that could be traced for many generations. One thing is for sure, George Washington did not like a bully king and he was not going to stand by when his king became a bully.

Even though George Washington's great grandfather came to the colonies in 1650, his family was very proud to be British citizens. Mr. Washington was born in Virginia in 1732. He was a very large baby who grew to be a very tall man for this time. Mr. Washington was homeschooled. He also worked very hard on his family's Ferry Farm. Many daily chores helped him grow up to be strong and hard working. Mr. Washington's father died when he was just eleven years old, and he had to become the "man of the house" at this very young age.

Mr. Washington did not grow up in a rich family. He was only able to "move up in society" after he married Martha Dandridge Custis. His brothers had left the home to start their own lives and he was the only man in the house to work the farm and provide for his family. As a teenager, he wrote a letter to his friend Henry Knox, and said he would love to go to the public dances in town, but he didn't have enough money to buy corn for his horse. He had to learn the value of hard work and responsibility to keep his farm and take care of his family. These lessons would be very important to him one day, as he led the people of the colonies in a very difficult battle for Liberty, and when he became the first President of the United States under the Constitution.

In 1753, Mr. Washington was very excited when it was his turn to join the militia of Virginia. He volunteered to travel over a thousand miles on horseback to deliver a message to the commander of the French Army. This message was from London, telling the commander that he must leave the Ohio valley immediately. Mr. Washington had asked some Native American's to help and guide him safely. He delivered the message and got a reply from the commander, and it was time for Mr. Washington to go back.

The weather had gotten really bad while he waited for the commander's reply and the rivers were frozen and the temperature was below zero. Mr. Washington and his friend had to cross a river that was full of ice, but not frozen. They spent all day making a raft to cross the river. But when they were half way, a huge piece of ice knocked Mr. Washington off of the raft into the icy river. He was able to pull himself back onto the raft, but was now soaking wet in below freezing temperatures. There was no way they could cross the river, so they found an island and spent the night in under a tree. They had no fire, no blankets, and no beds.

Because Mr. Washington was covered in water, the water shielded him from the freezing cold. Most of his friend's fingers and toes were frozen. By morning the river was totally frozen, and they were able to cross on foot and make back safely.

This would not be the last time Mr. Washington was miraculously saved in perilous times. Mr. Washington would often say he knew that the hand of God had protected him during his battles. In 17755 Washington was helping General Braddock fight the French, when General Braddock was killed George Washington he rode back and forth on across the battlefield rallying the troops until they could escape. He became known as a brave hero. A legend tells of an Indian Chief at this battle who said, in 1770, that Mr. Washington could not be killed in battle. The chief said that "the Great Spirit protects that man, and guides his destinies – he will become the chief of nations, and a people yet unborn will hail him as the founder of a mighty empire!" After one battle, Mr. Washington would find bullet holes in his coat and in his hat, but he was not injured. He believed that God was protecting him.

George. Washington would fight very hard so that America could have a chance to be the land of the free. And when Mr. Washington heard Patrick Henry say, "give me Liberty or give me death" he agreed that peace was not worth being a slave to the bully king. He spent his own money and used his own food and supplies to pay, feed, and clothe the soldiers during the Revolutionary War. He knew in his soul that when the king was acting like a bully, what he was really doing was making the colonists his slaves. Mr. Washington knew that God created men in his image, equal and free. He was willing to sacrifice everything so that people in the future could live free, and enjoy God's gift of Liberty.

Mr. Washington said many times that he knew God had a job for him to do. He knew that God kept him safe and gave him the ability to fight for Liberty. He would spend the rest of his life living for God and for the gift of Liberty. He was not only our first General, but our first President under the Constitution. He was not a member of a political party and hope that America would not form political parties. George Washington was a man of principle who listened to God and sacrificed everything knowing that God would protect him and honor his fight for Liberty. Mr. Washington and men like him gave everything so that America could be an exceptional nation!

Study Questions

1. Where did George Washington go to school?
2. How did George Washington become strong and learn to work hard?
3. What made George Washington believe that God was protecting him?
4. Did George Washington grow up rich?
5. To which political party did George Washington belong?

16 ARTICLES OF CONFEDERATION

Right after Richard Henry Lee wrote his plan the "Lee Resolution", the Second Continental Congress began writing the Articles of Confederation. The Articles were an agreement between the colonies to come together and fight the king and be one nation of states. They had to do this so the people would be able to fight the American Revolutionary War, ask other countries to help with the war and help the new states get along with each other and the Native Indians. It took the people a year to write the Articles of Confederation and then it took them another 4 years for the states to agree on the exact words. They knew this was a very important agreement. They did not want to create a new government just like the bully king's, so they made sure that this new government was very limited in power. Five years after the colonies said they would no longer be slaves to the bully king, the colonies had an agreement with each other to be united.

There were seven Presidents under the Articles of Confederation starting with John Hanson and ending with Cyrus Griffin. The most famous President is John Hancock, the guy with the big signature on the Declaration of Independence. The Articles of Confederation created a central government, but left the individual colonies, now called states, as free as possible from the rule of the central government. The people did not want to take the chance of creating a bully king but knew that a central government would be needed to organize the states and keep them safe from foreign enemies. They also wanted the central government to speak for the states to other countries so they could trade and buy things and make friends. The people started to notice that the central government was not working like they had wanted.

The central government had to organize and keep the states safe from enemy countries. But, the central government didn't collect any taxes so it had no money to do what the people wanted it to do. There was no money to pay people to represent the new America in talks with other countries. They had no money to buy or sell things with other countries. There was no court system to enforce the laws. There was no one to pay the Congressman or even organize meetings for them come to work. Things began to become very disorganized and very frustrating for the founders. They knew that something had to change if America was to stay a safe and free country.

The founders knew they did not want to create the opportunity for a bully king to rise up and take over America. They wanted to make sure that the states and the people kept all the power and the central government stayed very small and limited. There were many different ideas on how to do this. Two groups of people formed to discuss how this "more perfect union" would be created. Both groups wanted to make sure that America was a place where Liberty could grow, they just had different ideas on the best way to do that.

One group was called the Antifederalists. This group of people believed that a central government should stay very small and the states should keep most of the duties and most of the power. The person who wrote the Anti-Federalist paper number one said that they would be in favor of the new Constitution if it would guarantee Liberty to the people. The Antifederalists were very sure that if the new Constitution did not protect the Liberty of the people, they would make sure it was fixed before the people would vote to keep it. The Antifederalists believed guarding Liberty was more important than forming a central government. They often said that they would rather remain individual states, than to join a union that would become a bully king and put them into slavery once again.

The other group was called the Federalists. These people also believed that Liberty was the most important thing in forming the new American government. They also believed that if the states stayed separate that they would be in danger of foreign attack. Without a central government there would be no way to organize the states quickly to protect each other. The states would be beaten by the foreign governments, and the people would then be made the slaves of that government and Liberty would be lost. The Federalists believed the people must agree to give a central government more power than the Articles of Confederation. The central government had to have the power to collect taxes for the protection of the states and for making agreements with foreign countries. They said that the powers given to the central government would be very few. These powers would be limited to keeping peace with other countries, fighting wars, making agreements, and buying and selling with other countries. The main things that the people were wanted the states to be able to make decisions for themselves and they didn't want another bully government stealing Liberty.

These two groups of people worked very hard to give America the best chance to be a place where Liberty would grow. They had many discussions on the best way to keep Liberty and keep America safe at the same time. Both groups decided that Liberty was the most important thing. They knew that if they protected Liberty above everything else, they would be doing the best thing for America. They were able to come to an agreement that the Constitution was the best way to create a more perfect union. They had agreed on a way to make sure that Liberty would grow and make sure that the people would be free from a bully king telling them how to live their lives. Because our founders put Liberty first, they were able to write the Constitution of the United States, including the Bill of Rights, and give America the greatest chance of being an exceptional nation.

Study Questions

1. How many American Presidents served under the Articles of Confederation?
2. What was America's first Constitution called?
3. What was the problem that the founders later realized about the Articles of Confederation?
4. What was the main belief of the Antifederalists?
5. What were the two main things that the people wanted?

17 CONSTITUTION

The main way that America has protected Liberty is through the Constitution. Do you know what the Constitution is? Think about it like this:

When someone wants to build a house they have to make a plan. This plan is a drawing that tells the builders exactly how the house is supposed to be built. How long the boards are supposed to be...where the lights are supposed to go...where the cabinets will be. The Constitution tells us exactly how the government is supposed to be built. It also tells us how it's supposed to work – what it can do and what it can't do.

The States each sent representatives to write the Constitution, The States created the central government to do the jobs listed in the Constitution. If the federal government wants to know what it is supposed to do and what it is not supposed to do, it is supposed to look at its blueprint, the Constitution. Our founders knew it was very important to draw this plan in such a way that the government would have just the few jobs listed in the Constitution and the States, who created the government, would keep all the powers with the people. Our founders were so sure that the government needed to understand that Liberty was something that belonged to the people that they wrote the Bill of Rights, explaining a few of the most important rights that government is supposed to protect.

Some people thought that the Bill of Rights was not something that we should write down. Alexander Hamilton, one of our founding fathers, was worried that if we listed these rights, it would give the central government the chance to keep people from enjoying those rights. Mr. Hamilton said that if we write them down the evil men would try to tell the people what those rights meant and not what they really meant when God gave them to us. He believed that the government would change the meaning of those rights, act like a big bully and work hard to keep people from enjoying those rights.

The other people also didn't want the central government to be a big bully, but they had a different idea about the Bill of Rights. James Madison, another founding father, warned that if they did not list these very important rights, people might forget what they are. Mr. Madison knew that when people forget what their rights are, governments will become bullies and keep the people from enjoying those rights. He said that we must write down these very important rights in the Bill of Rights so we will remind the government of the rights they are to protect and remind the people to guard the rights that God has given them. The way that they tried to settle this issue was by including the 9th and 10th amendments, which are supposed to let the federal government know that they are not allowed to do anything accept what is written in the Constitution, if it is not written then it is not a power that they have. Any power not written in the Constitution belongs to the people in their states.

Most of our modern representatives, lawyers and judges have either forgotten what the 9th and 10th amendments are for or they just don't want to pay attention to them. One way that we can protect liberty is to make sure that our government follows the 9th and 10th amendments.

Both the Federalists and Antifederalists knew that since God gave us Liberty, no man or government could take them away, but when the people forget what their rights are, they can give them away and let bullies push them around. This was such an important part of protecting Liberty, these two groups of people talked about these differences for a very long time. They listened to each other's ideas and worked together to create the Constitution and Bill of Rights we have today. What we ended up with in the Constitution AND the Bill of Rights was a result of this important debate. This is one of the reasons it is so important to discuss and argue over why something works or doesn't. This kind of debate which is protected in America by our first amendment is one reason America is an exceptional nation.

Study Question

1. How is the Constitution like a blueprint to a house?
2. Who created the Constitution and therefore created the federal government?
3. Many were concerned that the central government would do more than it was supposed to do. Which two amendments to the Constitution were supposed to let the government know that it is limited?
4. What was Hamilton's worry about including a Bill of Rights?
5. Why did Madison say we must have a Bill of Rights?

18 CONCLUSION

What is it that makes America exceptional? One of our presidents, named Ronald Reagan said "I believe that God put this land between the two great oceans, to be found by special people from every corner of the world." We are a nation of people from all parts of the world and all walks of life. We know that Liberty is a very important gift from God. We know that God created everyone equal. We know that Liberty belongs to the people and it is the government's job to protect that liberty. We know that our future is limited only by our dreams and our hard work to make those dreams happen. America is an exceptional nation because it came from exceptional people.

America STILL HAS exceptional people. America is not perfect, because people are not perfect. Americans still believe what our founders believe. Liberty has not changed. A great founding father named Daniel Webster said "Hold on, my friends, to the Constitution and to the Republic for which it stands. Miracles do not cluster, and what has happened once in 6000 years, may not happen again." He was telling us that America is a great nation. America was built on the plan of Liberty by great people who believed in a great God. We cannot take that for granted. We must fight to keep Liberty. If we stop believing that America is exceptional, then America will become just like every other country. America will become a country that does not stand for Liberty.

But America is an exceptional nation because of our exceptional beliefs. Those beliefs are written in the documents our founders gave us - The Declaration of Independence, the Constitution and the Bill of Rights. Our founders learned those beliefs by studying over 700 years' worth of fighting to keep Liberty.

Our founders made America a nation that believes that all people are created equal, and that God gave all men rights that cannot be taken away from them. Our founders believed that all people had the right to life, liberty, freedom of religion, and the ability to own property. No other country loves Liberty, loves God, and loves people like America. People may tell you that America did not start out making all people free. That is true. But America is the only nation that was created to know Liberty is the most important thing.

Our sixteenth president, Abraham Lincoln, said America was "CONCEIVED in liberty, and DEDICATED to the proposition that all men are created equal". Our founders knew if they created a nation built with the plan of Liberty, people would see Liberty and want it for themselves. Our founders knew it would not be long before everyone enjoyed Liberty. Our founders gave us a way to share Liberty with everyone with the greatest plan for Liberty ever written. Americans know that Liberty is worth fighting for and that is what we do. We have to, because we are Americans and Liberty is who we are.

America is also exceptional because Americans believe in an exceptional God that protects us and His gift of Liberty. The Declaration of Independence says we are part of "the Laws of Nature and of Nature's God." It also says that we have a Creator that gives man Liberty. The Declaration of Independence makes a prayer to God to protect the people as we fight for Liberty.

Thomas Jefferson also prayed to God to help the people in their battle for Liberty. Mr. Jefferson also warned us that if we want to keep Liberty we must always remember that Liberty is a gift from God.

One of our founders named Benjamin Franklin reminded the people in Congress that they prayed to God all the time while they were fighting against the bully king. He asked them if they thought that they could make a new America that loved Liberty if they didn't pray to God all the time? Mr. Franklin warned them that they must always look to God for help and guidance if they wanted America to be an exceptional nation.

Patrick Henry said "Three millions of people, armed in the holy cause of liberty, and in such a country as that which we possess, are invincible by any force which our enemy can send against us. Besides, sir, we shall not fight our battles alone. There is a just God who presides over the destinies of nations, and who will raise up friends to fight our battles for us."

You see, our founders gave us a nation built on the plan of Liberty. They knew Liberty was so important that they had to fight against the bully kings. They knew that they could trust God to help them. But more than that, they wanted US to know how important Liberty is and that WE should trust God to help us. They wanted Americans to always fight against bully kings so that all people could be free. They wanted us to know that Liberty is more important that peace. They wanted us to know that bully kings will not allow people to have Liberty. They wanted us to know that America is an exceptional nation and Americans are an exceptional people.

About the Author

KrisAnne Hall is a Constitutional attorney and former state prosecutor, fired after teaching the Constitution to TEA Party groups - she would not sacrifice liberty for a paycheck. She is a disabled veteran of the US Army, a Russian linguist, a mother, a pastor's wife and a patriot. She now travels the country and teaches the Constitution and the history that gave us our founding documents. Awarded the Freedom Fighter award by Americans for Prosperity, and the Certificate of Achievement from the Sons of the Revolution for her defense of Constitutional principles, Congressman James Blair Award for Defense of the Constitution. Author of "Not a Living Breathing Document: Reclaiming Our Constitution, and the DVD series The Roots of Liberty: The Historic Foundations of The Bill of Rights. Two books that inspired KrisAnne's love for our history were Founding Brothers by Joseph Ellis and 1776 by David McCollough.

Born and raised in St. Louis, MO. She received her undergraduate degree in Bio-Chemistry from Blackburn College in 1991 and her J.D. from the University of Florida, Levin College of Law and is a former Russian Linguist for the US Army. KrisAnne now resides in North Florida with her husband Chris (a pastor and former Russian instructor for the US Navy) and her adopted son Colton. Visit her at **KrisAnneHall.com**

KrisAnne is an incredibly passionate speaker - a true Patrick Henry of our time. She speaks to audiences all across the country on Constitutional History, American Exceptionalism, and the Fight fror Liberty. Her passion and enthusiasm is contagious and she is able to inspire any group. A steadfast warrior in the Tea Party battle.

KrisAnne also teaches an incredible, MUST-SEE seminar on the Bill of Rights:

KrisAnne Hall's Bill of Rights Workshop, The Roots of Liberty is **NOT JUST ANOTHER LECTURE ON THE CONSTITUTION**. She presents the 700+ year history that gave us our founding documents - proving that our founding documents were not created on a whim and that they are reliable and relevant. It is is important to know not only what your rights are, but why you have them. In addition to the history of the Bill of Rights, KrisAnne presents each of the first ten amendments in their context - in the words and history of our founders. KrisAnne is a passionate speaker and has kept crowds attention for hours. This information is a must for all patriots and it must be passed on. If we are to reclaim our nation, we must reclaim our history! (The intro to the essential history of our founding documents is 1 hour, the full workshop is 5-6 hrs (1hr segments))

Available as a 3-DVD Set. Great for homeschool, church of grassroots instruction.

Here are a few testimonies:

Teenager from Winterhaven, FL - Your Teaching gave me goosebumps!

Lester from Lakeland, FL - As a person who has studied some history via the 5000yr Leap and the Making of American, I must say I have learned so much more in this first hour of your video.

Ray from Kaufman, TX - I have a BS degree in History from a Texas University. I **learned more** about the Constitution **in an hour**, than in 4 years of college.

James from Miami - **I thought I knew the Constitution.** This seminar made me realize that if you don't know the history and you don't know what our founders said and meant, then you DON'T know the Constitution.

Gloria from Smith Co., Texas - I attended your workshop in Tyler at the Air Museum yesterday. I am totally blown away. **How much I did not know** and understand about the history of the framing of the Bill of Rights, **and I have attended three workshops prior to this one**

Mike from Atlanta - This is EXACTLY the **building blocks** we are going to need **to rebuild this nation**. In fact these are the only building blocks that will work. AMAZING PRESENTATION!!!! I could have listened for 12 hours!

Amanda from Putnam Co., FL - KrisAnne, you truly are **an amazing teacher!** After you spoke at our Tea Party meeting in Putnam County last week, we all left feeling renewed in our fight for liberty! I ordered your book last night and I cannot wait to read it!**Thank you for inspiring me.**

9.12 Member Tallahassee - To be honest, I have all but given up on this nation - it just seems like a losing battle sometimes. And I am convinced that eventually America will fall - the whole "there is no USA in the book of Revelation" thing - and you can't change prophecy - so I guess it'll be sooner than later and there's nothing that I can do about it. This has been a huge source of heartache and frustration for me. But tonight, **I have regained hope for our nation** -and here's why:

The truths that you spoke tonight were, in my eyes, profound- some of which I have heard in the past from previous research - many of the historical truths were new to me. And that was all great. But as I sat tonight listening to you, I felt the presence of the Holy Spirit. You are truly anointed to speak on this topic - to proclaim this message from the housetops. Of that hat I have no doubt. And so it's not the truths in themselves that give me hope - but that God has anointed you to deliver this message - and if God has anointed someone to deliver a message, it's not without a purpose. So **there must be hope in restoring this nation**. That is where my new hope has come from - the fact that **this message is anointed**.

Thank you so for answering this call. I know it's not easy. To whom much is given, much is required... and it will not be without great reward.

Robert from St. Augustine - Thank you so much for your remarks at the St. Augustine Tea Party last night. Your defense of our Constitution and liberty through freedom and faith was both **inspiring**and **educational**. Thank you so much for what you are doing for our country and the State of Florida. God Save the Republic.

Ken from Pembroke Pines, FL - I enjoyed and learned from your speech... I am a lawyer...If there is any opportunity to work with you or learn from you, please **count me in**.

Donna from Broward TEA Party, FL - Krisanne I want to say thank you for your service to our country. As much as any service man or woman fighting for our country, you are fighting for all of us. I saw and heard you speak at the Broward County

Tea Party meeting this past Wednesday. Your presentation was **so inspiring**. I bought your CD package and I just finished watching it. I had planned to wait and watch it with my son and grandsons but couldn't wait. I will gladly **watch it again** with them. It is so sad that every person in our country can't have the opportunity to attend one of your presentations. I just know it would open so many eyes and hearts. I will be telling everyone I have contact with to check out your website and to try to hear you speak if they can. Thank you again for all that you are doing for our country.

Karen and Butch from Panola Co., Texas - We enjoyed/leaned so much from your seminar/lesson/mission. We will share and are grateful what you shared with us...We have your book, your Bill of Rights DVD's, and your CD on The Roots of Liberty. Now we have your web site. We are going to work hard to share all you taught us. Thank you.

Made in the USA
Charleston, SC
22 February 2014